JAXON AND KIWI ROAD SAFETY

Jaxon and Kiwi Road Safety

Tanika Stimpson

Jaxon Stimpson

Jaxon and Kiwi

Jaxon is a young boy with Type 1 diabetes. Jaxon is constantly learning new skills that will help him in life, not only to stay safe but to also keep his buddy Kiwi safe. Kiwi is Jaxon's medical assistant dog who alerts him to low sugars and comforts him during diabetes set changes as it can be a lot for him.

Kiwi training
Tanika

Jaxon and Kiwi are constantly learning new skills every day. Kiwi has learned how to find Jaxon's glucose monitor to bring the monitor to Jaxon when he needs it. That's not all, Jaxon and Kiwi have been learning about Road Safety this is an important skill to learn. Jaxon learnt that when he hops out of the car he has to put his hand on the safety sticker.

When Jaxon and Kiwi walk together each morning and afternoon around their community they practice road safety. They look both ways and wait for Mum to say it's ok to cross. Jaxon holds Kiwi's lead or his handle on his harness and Mum holds Kiwi's lead on the opposite side.

When at the road Jaxon stands next to Mum and Kiwi. While standing at the road Kiwi practices pressing the button to cross the road, and when he does Kiwi is so happy. Once Kiwi presses the button he sits by the road waiting for the crossing light to change to green.

Kiwi pressing button

As Kiwi presses the button he then waits at the road listening to the traffic, and looking up at Mum to ensure it's safe to cross.

Waiting to cross the street

Jaxon and Kiwi have also been practising stopping when near the road and looking left and right, they then tell mum if they see a car coming.

While out in the street, Jaxon and Kiwi learn about sharing the footpath with others. When Jaxon and Kiwi see people and other children approaching Jaxon and Kiwi listen to their mum. when she tells them to move out of the other people's way they step to the side and watch them pass by sometimes Kiwi waves to the kids passing by.

They also learn that when on a bike or scooter to allow people to pass and not do tricks too close to people as it can hurt someone.

RESOURCES

Parent Resources

These are some websites to visit to gain tips on how to teach road safety they include videos that can be shared with your children.

- Kidsafe NSW Road Safety
- RaisingChildren.net.au (pedestrian safety and road safety)
- Constable Kenny (constablekenny.org.au)

COLOUR

Do you know what this road sign is?
Can you colour this in.

Traffic lights
Super colouring

COLOUR

Do you know What sign this is?
Lets colour this picture

Pedestrian crossing ahead
https://www.supercoloring.com/coloring-pages/
pedestrian-crossing-ahead-sign-in-australia

Do you know what this sign is?
Can you colour this in.

Children crossing sign
Super colouring

About the author.

I'm a solo mum to a Type 1 Diabetic child and his diabetes assistant dog. I had decided to start writing children's books for my son as I didn't see many books about diabetes assistant dogs. Being a Diploma-trained Early Childhood Educator, I also wanted to make educational books for young minds. Once we received our diabetes assistance dog I started to write my first book called "Jaxon and Kiwi Adventures".

Being a diabetes mum has been hard work especially learning how to deal with it but what got me through it all was seeing my child being brave and dealing with it all. I have written many blogs.